T0195716

If You Miss the Rapture

The Savior's Perspective

Luke Hendrickson

WESTBOW
P R E S S®
A DIVISION OF THOMAS NELSON
& ZONDERVAN

Scripture taken from the King James Version of the Bible.

WestBow Press books may be ordered through booksellers or by contacting:

WestBow Press
A Division of Thomas Nelson & Zondervan
1663 Liberty Drive
Bloomington, IN 47403
www.westbowpress.com
1 (866) 928-1240

ISBN: 978-1-9736-0140-1 (sc)
ISBN: 978-1-9736-0139-5 (hc)
ISBN: 978-1-9736-0141-8 (e)

Library of Congress Control Number: 2017913143

Print information available on the last page.

WestBow Press rev. date: 8/30/2017

Contents

Preface

No one knows the day or the hour when the Lord Jesus will return for His church. Do not listen to those who set dates on when the Rapture will occur.

> **But of that day and [that] hour knoweth no man, no, not the angels which are in heaven, neither the Son, but the Father. Take ye heed, watch and pray: for ye know not when the time is. ... Lest coming suddenly he find you sleeping. And what I say unto you I say unto all, Watch. (Mark 13:32–33, 36–37)**

The key points Jesus emphasized is that we do not know when the Rapture will take place and that His bride should be ready.

And while they went to buy, the bridegroom came; and they that were ready went in with him to the marriage: and the door was shut. Afterward came also the other virgins, saying, Lord, Lord, open to us. But he answered and said, Verily I say unto you, I know you not. Watch therefore, for ye know neither the day nor the hour wherein the Son of man cometh. (Matthew 25:10–13)

This book will focus on the church getting ready for His return; let us not play games with God. Jesus is coming back after a bride without spot or blemish. After He gets His bride, the door will be shut. May we be ready when He comes.

All scripture references are from the King James Version of the Bible.

Chapter 1

Recognizing the Spirit of the Antichrist

We believers must realize that the spirit of the Antichrist has been on earth for a very long time.

Little children, it is the last time: and as ye have heard that antichrist shall come, even now are there many antichrists; whereby we know that it is the last time. (1 John 2:18)

And every spirit that confesseth not that Jesus Christ is come in the flesh is not of God: and this is that [spirit] of antichrist, whereof ye have heard that it should come; and even now already is it in the world. (1 John 4:3)

The man of sin, the Antichrist or the abomination of desolation, could already be here on the earth though he has not been revealed yet. His spirit has been here since the first deception in the Garden of Eden. We need to understand the biblical meaning of who the Antichrist is and how that spirit deceives to be able to recognize him.

> **Who is a liar but he that denieth that Jesus is the Christ? He is antichrist, that denieth the Father and the Son. Whosoever denieth the Son, the same hath not the Father: [but] he that acknowledgeth the Son hath the Father also. (1 John 2:22–23)**

If someone says Jesus is not the Christ, it should be very easy to recognize the spirit behind that statement. However, the devil and his seducing spirits will always try to change what the Word of God says; this is not always easy to recognize. Satan will always try to complicate things. He will say things like "hath God said," just as he did in Genesis 3.

> **Now the serpent was more subtle than any beast of the field which the Lord God had made. And he said unto the woman, Yea, hath God said, Ye shall not eat of every tree of the garden. (Genesis 3:1)**

Often, the first thing Satan will do is try to complicate what the Word of God has put in simple terms such as "Don't eat of this fruit." No matter how he starts trying to get people thinking wrong, he will try to lead them to conclude, "It's okay if I disobey God." All the devil's lies are rooted in this. If we buy into this lie, we cannot please God.

Let's take a closer look at the definition of Antichrist: "A great adversary of Christ; the man of sin; described in a more general sense, the word extends to any persons who deny Christ or oppose the fundamental doctrines of Christianity." If at any time the fundamentals of the gospel are changed, we change whom we are talking about. When we change the Word of God, we are changing to another Jesus that suits our lifestyle. Instead, we should let Jesus change us. One of the major ways of thinking that is opposed to the fundamental doctrines of Christianity is: a gospel of works that produces salvation.

Believing we are saved by what we do will never get us to heaven. We must put our faith exclusively in the cross of Christ.

> **For by grace are ye saved through faith; and that not of yourselves: [it is] the gift of God: Not of works, lest any man should boast. (Ephesians 2:8–9)**

If you ask average people if they are going to heaven when they die, most of them will say, "I think so." If you ask them why they think so, they will likely say something like "Well, I'm a pretty good person." They are depending on the wrong thing to save them. The spirit of the Antichrist is behind this type of belief system. Many people think it doesn't matter what religion they are; they think God will accept them as long as they are good even if they don't put their faith in Jesus. This belief is the beginning of the push to one-world religion. The spirit of the Antichrist is definitely behind this.

Most religions will agree that Jesus is a prophet. The major problem they have with us Christians is when we say Jesus is the only way to the Father. A true prophet cannot be a liar. Jesus told the truth because He is the way, the truth, and the life.

Jesus saith unto him, "I am the way, the truth, and the life: no man cometh unto the Father, but by me." (John 14:6)

We need to look at what is the major form of deception the spirit of the Antichrist is using in the Christian church today. It goes back to the original sin and deception in the Garden of Eden when sin entered into the world. We can look at what happened between the serpent and Eve from all possible angles. No matter how we look at it, what the devil got her to believe is, "It's okay if I disobey God." This belief has infected the modern church; this is why we see very prominent Christian leaders getting caught repeatedly in blatant sin.

When we change the fundamentals of the gospel, we are preaching another Jesus. Even in his day, the apostle Paul had a fear of this happening in the churches he had planted. This goes right back to the very first deception.

But I fear, lest by any means, as the serpent beguiled Eve through his subtilty, so your minds should be corrupted from the simplicity that is in Christ. For if he that cometh preacheth another Jesus, whom we have not preached, or [if] ye receive another spirit, which ye have not received, or another gospel, which ye have not accepted, ye might well bear with [him]. (2 Corinthians 11:3–4)

True biblical salvation is followed by the amendment of life and good works we perform not to be saved but because we are saved. We must continually renew our minds and lives by obeying and living by the Word of God; this means being obedient to God. Don't buy the lie that it's okay to disobey God.

Too many times, people think the grace of God allows them to live sinful lifestyles; this belief comes straight from the spirit of the Antichrist. I have heard many definitions of grace, one of which is "unmerited favor." This is definitely a big part of the definition. The grace of God is the power of God working in us to do what we have no power to do ourselves. The grace of God gives us the power to continually come out of sin and live obedient lives that are pleasing to God. Thank God that His mercies are new every morning. Thank God that He gives us the grace—the power—we need to obey Him.

Jesus is our perfect example of obedience. Jesus is the Son of God, and He had to learn obedience. We must purpose in our hearts to follow His example.

> **Though he were a Son, yet learned he obedience by the things which he suffered; And being made perfect, he became the author of eternal salvation unto all them that obey him. (Hebrews 5:8–9)**

Living a life in obedience to God is a requirement of faith in Christ. New believers need to understand this when they make professions of faith in Christ. They need to understand what it means when they confess Jesus as Lord of their lives.

That if thou shalt confess with thy mouth the Lord Jesus, and shalt believe in thine heart that God hath raised him from the dead, thou shalt be saved. (Romans 10:9)

Confessing Jesus as Lord means that He is the boss and that we must do what He says.

And why call ye me, Lord, Lord, and do not the things which I say? (Luke 6:46)

If we truly love Jesus, we will keep His commandments. The spirit of Antichrist would say, "Only believe," but believing properly brings obedience.

If ye love me, keep my commandments ... He that hath my commandments, and keepeth them, he it is that loveth me: and he that loveth me shall be loved of my Father, and I will love him, and will manifest myself to him ... Jesus answered and said unto him, If a man love me, he will keep my words: and my Father will love him, and we will come unto him, and make our abode with him. He that loveth me not keepeth not my sayings: and the word which ye hear is not mine, but the Father's which sent me. (John 14:15, 21, 23–24)

These are not my words but those of God the Father's. Obedience is a requirement and necessary fruit of our faith. If we have no fruit, we have no foundational root.

In 1 John, we find a lot instruction on living lives in obedience to God. One phrase that I am beginning to hear in the modern church is that Jesus forgives all our sins—past, present, and future—when we are saved. There is some truth in this statement as far as our eternal salvation is concerned. However, this type of theology may leave people with the idea, "If I sin, God already knew I would, so why should I confess it and forsake it?" They likely will begin to think, It's okay if I disobey God.

Let's look at some verses in 1 John that will help us realize we need to remain faithful to Christ. The first thing we need to understand about John's letter is to whom it was written.

> **I write unto you, little children, because your sins are forgiven you for his name's sake. I write unto you, fathers, because ye have known him [that is] from the beginning. I write unto you, young men, because ye have overcome the wicked one. I write unto you, little children, because ye have known the Father. (1 John 2:12–13)**

One of the main reasons this letter was written was for believers to have fullness of joy. Some of the most miserable people on earth could be Christians who are not living lives in submission to the will of God for their lives.

> **And these things write we unto you, that your joy may be full. (1 John 1:4)**

If we are going to have fellowship and joy in God, we have to walk in the light He is continually revealing to us. If we say we know Him but continue to live a sinful life style and walk in darkness, we are liars.

If we say that we have fellowship with him, and walk in darkness, we lie, and do not the truth. (1 John 1:6)

As believers who are still being conformed to the image of Christ, we must through the Spirit put to death the sinful desires lurking in our mortal bodies. We are to be continually walking in the light the Spirit of God is revealing to us. There is nothing good in these bodies other than the spirit God placed in us when we were born again. Many times, there may be flaws in our character that amount to sin in our lives that we may not even be aware of. But if we walk in the light that we have, the blood of Jesus cleanses us from those sins as well. If, however, we think we have achieved sinless perfection, we deceive ourselves.

> **But if we walk in the light, as he is in the light, we have fellowship one with another, and the blood of Jesus Christ his Son cleanseth us from all sin. If we say that we have no sin, we deceive ourselves, and the truth is not in us. If we confess our sins, he is faithful and just to forgive us [our] sins, and to cleanse us from all unrighteousness. If we say that we have not sinned, we**

make him a liar, and his word is not in us. (1 John 1:7–10)

When the Spirit of God reveals sin to us, we need to confess that sin to Him and forsake it. When we do, it's over with—God doesn't even remember that sin. But if we think we are already forgiven, why would we need to confess them? Why did John write these things to us? We find the answer in the next verse.

> **My little children, these things write I unto you, that ye sin not. And if any man sin, we have an advocate with the Father, Jesus Christ the righteous. (1 John 2:1)**

> **In this book, the apostle John told how we could know that we know God.**

> **And hereby we do know that we know him, if we keep his commandments. He that saith, I know him, and keepeth not his commandments, is a liar, and the truth is not in him. (1 John 2:3–4)**

> **As believers, we must realize we cannot let sin have dominion over us.**

For sin shall not have dominion over you: for ye are not under the law, but under grace [grace is the power that gives us the victory over sin]. What then? shall we sin, because we are not under the law, but under grace? God forbid. 16 Know ye not, that to whom ye yield yourselves servants to obey, his servants ye are to whom ye obey; whether of sin unto death, or of obedience unto righteousness? (Romans 6:14–16)

The spirit of the Antichrist would have us believe that we cannot gain victory over sin and that it's okay if we don't. Don't buy it—we are more than conquerors through Christ.

I have a confident expectation and hope that this chapter will help you understand that the spirit of Antichrist is already working in the earth (1 John 2:18, 4:3). I hope you understand that only faith in Jesus Christ can save you. There are no ways to heaven except through Jesus Christ. The only works you can depend on to save you is what Jesus did through His life, death, burial, and resurrection. I hope you understand all the devil's lies are rooted in the first example found in scripture— disobedience to God is okay. I hope you understand that Jesus Christ has given you the victory over the world, the flesh, and the devil. I hope you understand true biblical salvation is followed by an amended life and good works.

Chapter 2

Repentance–The Message to the Modern, Last-Days Church

Why is sin so prevalent in the modern church? Why do we see mainline Christian denominations performing same-sex marriages and even ordaining homosexual ministers? Why is divorce among Christians so high, sometimes even higher than it is among non-Christians? One of the main reasons is that repentance is no longer preached in our churches.

The message of repentance must be a common thread when the gospel of Jesus Christ is preached. We find the message of repentance throughout the New Testament from the beginning to end. People need to understand a wide variety of subject matter that we find in scripture, things such as grace and faith—the list could go on and on. I believe that the message of repentance, however, has been somewhat neglected by the modern church.

If we are to understand how important the message of repentance is in presenting the gospel, we first need to understand its definition.

> **Repentance, noun 2. In theology, the pain, regret or affliction which a person feels on account of his past conduct, because it exposes him to punishment. This sorrow proceeding merely from the fear of punishment is called legal repentance as being excited by the terrors of legal penalties, and it may exist without an amendment of life. 3. Real penitence; sorrow or deep contrition for sin, as an offense and dishonor to God, a violation of his holy law, and the basest ingratitude towards a Being of infinite benevolence.**

This is called evangelical repentance and is followed by an amendment of our lives. Repentance is a change of mind, a conversion from sin to God. Godly sorrow worketh repentance to salvation (2 Corinthians 7:9; Matthew 3:8). Repentance is the relinquishing of any practice that offends God.

In those days came John the Baptist, preaching in the wilderness of Judaea, And saying, Repent ye: for the kingdom of heaven is at hand. (Matthew 3:1–2)

John the Baptist was preparing the way for Jesus in these verses. The core of John's message was one of repentance.

From that time Jesus began to preach, and to say, Repent: for the kingdom of heaven is at hand. (Matthew 4:17)

In the next chapter in Matthew, Jesus confirmed the message given to John—repent.

Then opened he their understanding, that they might understand the scriptures, And said unto them, Thus it is written, and thus it behoved Christ to suffer, and to rise from the dead the third day: And that repentance and remission of sins should be preached in his name among all nations, beginning at Jerusalem. And ye are witnesses of these things. (Luke 24:45–48)

In the previous verses, Jesus told us that we were to present the gospel to all nations and that repentance must be a big part of the message. He has not changed. Have we? The modern church has to go back to preaching repentance—turning us from our wicked ways.

> **If my people, which are called by my name, shall humble themselves, and pray, and seek my face, and turn from their wicked ways; then will I hear from heaven, and will forgive their sin, and will heal their land. (2 Chronicles 7:14)**

If we are not preaching repentance in our churches, we are not preaching the message Jesus commissioned us to preach. We need the message of repentance preached in love in our churches in these last days.

The apostle Paul understood the importance of the message of repentance.

> **[And] how I kept back nothing that was profitable [unto you], but have shewed you, and have taught you publickly, and from house to house, Testifying both to the Jews, and also to the Greeks, repentance toward God, and faith toward our Lord Jesus Christ. (Acts 20:20–21)**

One of the first works of the Holy Spirit is to reprove or convict sinners of their sin. Then He will draw them to the cross of Christ and plead with them to accept Jesus's payment for their sin.

> **Nevertheless I tell you the truth; It is expedient for you that I go away: for if I go not away, the Comforter will not come unto you; but if I depart, I will send him unto you. And when he is come, he will reprove the world of sin, and of righteousness, and of judgment. (John 16:7–8)**

Pastors led by the Spirit of God will turn His people from their wickedness and evil ways.

> **But if they had stood in my counsel, and had caused my people to hear my words, then they should have turned them from their evil way, and from the evil of their doings. (Jeremiah 23:22)**

A very big part of the pastor's job in the modern church is to correct and reprove.

> **Preach the word; be instant in season, out of season; reprove, rebuke, exhort**

**with all longsuffering and doctrine.
(2 Titus 4:2)**

Being longsuffering means being very patient with people we are ministering to. Even when we are correcting and reproving people, they must hear love, gentleness, and concern in our voices. We must never preach at them because we are aggravated. We must always speak the truth in love, to help grow them up (Ephesians 4:11–15).

**And the servant of the Lord must not strive; but be gentle unto all [men], apt to teach, patient, In meekness instructing those that oppose themselves; if God peradventure will give them repentance to the acknowledging of the truth; And [that] they may recover themselves out of the snare of the devil, who are taken captive by him at his will.
(2 Timothy 2:24–26)**

If pastors will not preach what God has told them to, how can their congregations be ready when the Father sends Jesus for His bride? Repentance has to be a big part of the message to the modern church if its members are going to be ready for the Rapture. In this chapter, we have seen that Jesus and John the Baptist came out preaching repentance. The disciples continued with the same.

We will look at some verses in the book of Revelation on repentance. The Lord God Almighty had a message to the seven churches in Asia, and the major theme was repentance. He hasn't changed.

Unto the angel of the church of Ephesus write; These things saith he that holdeth the seven stars in his right hand, who walketh in the midst of the seven golden candlesticks; I know thy works, and thy labour, and thy patience, and how thou canst not bear them which are evil: and thou hast tried them which say they are apostles, and are not, and hast found them liars: And hast borne, and hast patience, and for my name's sake hast laboured, and hast not fainted. Nevertheless I have [somewhat] against thee, because thou hast left thy first love. Remember therefore from whence thou art fallen, and repent, and do the first works; or else I will come unto thee quickly, and will remove thy candlestick out of his place, except thou repent. But this thou hast, that thou hatest the deeds of the Nicolaitans, which I also hate. He that hath an ear, let him hear what

the Spirit saith unto the churches;
To him that overcometh will I give to
eat of the tree of life, which is in the
midst of the paradise of God.

And unto the angel of the church in
Smyrna write; These things saith the
first and the last, which was dead,
and is alive; I know thy works, and
tribulation, and poverty, (but thou
art rich) and [I know] the blasphemy
of them which say they are Jews,
and are not, but [are] the synagogue
of Satan. Fear none of those things
which thou shalt suffer: behold, the
devil shall cast [some] of you into
prison, that ye may be tried; and ye
shall have tribulation ten days: be
thou faithful unto death, and I will
give thee a crown of life. He that hath
an ear, let him hear what the Spirit
saith unto the churches; He that
overcometh shall not be hurt of the
second death.

And to the angel of the church in
Pergamos write; These things saith
he which hath the sharp sword with
two edges; I know thy works, and

where thou dwellest, [even] where Satan's seat [is]: and thou holdest fast my name, and hast not denied my faith, even in those days wherein Antipas [was] my faithful martyr, who was slain among you, where Satan dwelleth. But I have a few things against thee, because thou hast there them that hold the doctrine of Balaam, who taught Balac to cast a stumblingblock before the children of Israel, to eat things sacrificed unto idols, and to commit fornication. So hast thou also them that hold the doctrine of the Nicolaitans, which thing I hate. Repent; or else I will come unto thee quickly, and will fight against them with the sword of my mouth. He that hath an ear, let him hear what the Spirit saith unto the churches;

To him that overcometh will I give to eat of the hidden manna, and will give him a white stone, and in the stone a new name written, which no man knoweth saving he that receiveth [it].

And unto the angel of the church in Thyatira write; These things saith the Son of God, who hath his eyes like unto a flame of fire, and his feet [are] like fine brass; I know thy works, and charity, and service, and faith, and thy patience, and thy works; and the last [to be] more than the first. Notwithstanding I have a few things against thee, because thou sufferest that woman Jezebel, which calleth herself a prophetess, to teach and to seduce my servants to commit fornication, and to eat things sacrificed unto idols. And I gave her space to repent of her fornication; and she repented not. Behold, I will cast her into a bed, and them that commit adultery with her into great tribulation, except they repent of their deeds.

And I will kill her children with death; and all the churches shall know that I am he which searcheth the reins and hearts: and I will give unto every one of you according to your works. But unto you I say, and unto the rest in Thyatira, as many as have not this doctrine, and which have not known the depths of Satan, as they speak; I will put upon you none other burden. But that which ye have [already] hold fast till I come. And he that overcometh, and keepeth my works unto the end, to him will I give power over the nations: And he shall rule them with a rod of iron; as the vessels of a potter shall they be broken to shivers: even as I received of my Father. And I will give him the morning star. He that hath an ear, let him hear what the Spirit saith unto the churches.

And unto the angel of the church in Sardis write; These things saith he that hath the seven Spirits of God, and the seven stars; I know thy works, that thou hast a name that thou livest, and art dead. Be watchful, and strengthen the things which remain, that are ready to die: for I have not found thy works perfect before God. Remember therefore how thou hast received and heard, and hold fast, and repent. If therefore thou shalt not watch, I will come on thee as a thief, and thou shalt not know what hour I will come upon thee. Thou hast a few names even in Sardis which have not defiled their garments; and they shall walk with me in white: for they are worthy. He that overcometh, the same shall be clothed in white raiment; and I will not blot out his name out of the book of life, but I will confess his name before my Father, and before his angels. He that hath an ear, let him hear what the Spirit saith unto the churches.

And to the angel of the church in Philadelphia write; These things saith he that is holy, he that is true, he that hath the key of David, he that openeth, and no man shutteth; and shutteth, and no man openeth; I know thy works: behold, I have set before thee an open door, and no man can shut it: for thou hast a little strength, and hast kept my word, and hast not denied my name. Behold, I will make them of the synagogue of Satan, which say they are Jews, and are not, but do lie; behold, I will make them to come and worship before thy feet, and to know that I have loved thee. Because thou hast kept the word of my patience, I also will keep thee from the hour of temptation, which shall come upon all the world, to try them that dwell upon the earth. Behold, I come quickly: hold that fast which thou hast, that no man take thy crown.

Him that overcometh will I make a pillar in the temple of my God, and he shall go no more out: and I will write upon him the name of my God, and the name of the city of my God, [which is] new Jerusalem, which cometh down out of heaven from my God: and [I will write upon him] my new name. He that hath an ear, let him hear what the Spirit saith unto the churches.

And unto the angel of the church of the Laodiceans write; These things saith the Amen, the faithful and true witness, the beginning of the creation of God; I know thy works, that thou art neither cold nor hot: I would thou wert cold or hot. So then because thou art lukewarm, and neither cold nor hot, I will spue thee out of my mouth. Because thou sayest, I am rich, and increased with goods, and have need of nothing; and knowest not that thou art wretched, and miserable, and poor, and blind, and naked: I counsel thee to buy of me gold tried in the fire, that thou mayest be rich; and white raiment, that thou mayest be clothed, and [that] the shame of thy nakedness do not appear; and anoint thine eyes with eyesalve, that thou mayest see. As many as I love, I rebuke and chasten: be zealous therefore, and repent. Behold, I stand at the door, and knock: if any man hear my voice, and open the door, I will come in to him, and will sup with him, and he with me. To him that overcometh will I grant to sit with me in my throne, even as I also overcame, and am set down with my Father in his throne. He that hath an ear, let him hear what the Spirit saith unto the churches. (Rev. 2:1-29, 3:1-22)

It should be very clear through reading Revelation 2–3 what the Spirit was saying to the last-days church. It is very obvious that one of the main parts of the message is repentance. This message has not changed.

As believers, we are to continue the mind-renewal process to God's way of thinking. This comes by receiving the engrafted Word of God with meekness and being prompt to do what it says—letting the Holy Spirit and the Word of God continually mold us into the image of Christ; that will transform our lives; this is our reasonable service (Romans 12:1–2). We will never be able to do this if we buy the devil's first lie, "It's okay if I disobey God," or if we think too highly of ourselves. We must be willing to be changed from glory to glory by thinking differently. This is biblical repentance, and it accompanies true salvation. We must purpose in our hearts to remain faithful to Christ no matter the cost. All true believers endure to the end.

If someone quits on God, it may surprise you, it may surprise me, it may surprise a lot of people, but it will not surprise God.

Nevertheless the foundation of God standeth sure, having this seal, The Lord knoweth them that are his. And, Let every one that nameth the name of Christ depart from iniquity. (2 Timothy 2:19)

May we let the Word and Spirit of God change the way we think and live lives of submission to the will of God and depart from iniquity. This is biblical repentance.

I hope that after reading this chapter, you understand the message to the church of the last days—repent. Do you have ears to hear?

Chapter 3

He's Coming Back

As I have already stated in the preface to this book, the main points Jesus continues to make to His bride is: We don't know the day or the hour of His return; therefore, we should watch, pray, and be ready. If in any way what we believe about the end times, including the Rapture of the church, contradicts these basic principles, we need to take a close look at what we believe. Our belief must be based solely on the Word of God, not anyone's opinion.

In Matthew 24–25, Jesus described to His disciples the things that would occur on earth before His return. The first thing He said to them was to be careful not to be deceived. There is no doubt Jesus is right; a lot of deception is happening on earth about many things but especially about the return of Christ.

As ministers of God, we must lead God's people out of deception so they can be ready for Christ's return. I pray no one will be unprepared for His return and miss the Rapture because the door will be shut (Matthew 25:10). We must be obedient to God in doing this.

In no way do I want to sound condescending, judgmental, or critical about anyone who has a different view; that's in God's hands. I know the grace and forgiveness God has shown me when He has corrected me. I can only hope for that same grace to be shown to others who are in error.

Some of the main points I will bring out will disagree with a lot of the popular theology about the end times. All I ask you to do is compare what you may have been taught in scripture. The core of the error that will be exposed is this—people can live lives disobedient to God, reject the gospel, and still get into heaven after the Rapture. This is a very dangerous and false theology.

I want to focus on some key verses in Matthew to make some points very clear. The first point that Jesus made when asked about His return was for us to be cautious not to be deceived.

> **And Jesus answered and said unto them, Take heed that no man deceive you. For many shall come in my name, saying, I am Christ; and shall deceive many. (Matthew 24:4–5)**

Many people have a misunderstanding about this verse; they think it is speaking of the false prophets who have claimed to be the Christ. If that were the case, it would have to read like this: "For many shall come in my name saying they are Christ, and shall deceive many." The false prophets this verse is speaking about are those who will change the fundamentals of the gospel.

The devil's first lie, "It's okay if you disobey God," is at the core of their teaching. These false prophets will get many points of the gospel correct, but they will leave out some key points—things such as repentance, amendment of life, bearing fruit, and obedience to God in doing His will. They will have a form of godliness but deny the power thereof. Some of these false prophets will even perform same-sex marriages and ordain homosexual ministers in the name of Jesus Christ, turning the grace of God into a license to sin.

If we, the bride of Christ, will be ready for the Rapture, we must settle some things. We must continue to let the Word of God change us from glory to glory. We must live by the Word of God. He is coming back for a bride not having a spot, blemish, wrinkle, or any such thing. We must be living holy lives and show the love of God to a sinful world that will hate us.

> **That he might sanctify and cleanse it with the washing of water by the word, That he might present it to himself a glorious church, not having spot, or wrinkle, or any such thing;**

but that it should be holy and without blemish. (Ephesians 5:26–27)

Jesus had a lot to say in Matthew 24 about what would be going on before His return. I feel the need to emphasize this: you need to read the Word of God for yourself. If you are not going to be deceived, this is a must. Too many times, people live by every word that proceeds from the mouths of their favorite preachers instead of the written Word of God. If you won't read and study the Bible, how can you know if the preacher you like is right?

Let's look at some more verses in Matthew. They will no doubt shed some light on the very prevalent and dangerous false teaching that is infecting the airwaves on a global scale as well as the local church.

For as in the days that were before the flood they were eating and drinking, marrying and giving in marriage, until the day that Noe entered into the ark, And knew not until the flood came, and took them all away; so shall also the coming of the Son of man be. (Matthew 24:38–39)

Jesus was drawing a comparison between the last days before the Rapture and the days before the flood of Noah. The ark was a type of the Rapture. God was getting His people into the safety of the ark before His wrath was poured out. When the flood came, no one else was allowed to enter the ark because the Lord had shut the door.

> **And they went in unto Noah into the ark, two and two of all flesh, wherein [is] the breath of life. And they that went in, went in male and female of all flesh, as God had commanded him: and the LORD shut him in. (Genesis 7:15–16)**

After stating all that was mentioned in Matthew 24 about what to look for before the return of Christ, the scripture paints a very clear picture in the next chapter of what is expected of His bride. Be ready, because afterward, the door will be shut just as the ark's door was shut.

> **Then shall the kingdom of heaven be likened unto ten virgins, which took their lamps, and went forth to meet the bridegroom. And five of them were wise, and five [were] foolish. They that [were] foolish took their lamps, and took no oil with them: But the wise took oil in their vessels with their lamps. While the bridegroom tarried, they all slumbered and slept. And at midnight there was a cry made, Behold, the bridegroom cometh; go ye out to meet him. Then**

all those virgins arose, and trimmed their lamps. And the foolish said unto the wise, Give us of your oil; for our lamps are gone out.

But the wise answered, saying, [Not so]; lest there be not enough for us and you: but go ye rather to them that sell, and buy for yourselves. And while they went to buy, the bridegroom came; and they that were ready went in with him to the marriage: and the door was shut. (Matthew 25:1–10)

Jesus made it very clear that His bride must be ready for His return; if they miss the Rapture, the door of opportunity will be shut. The following verses make this point even clearer.

Afterward came also the other virgins, saying, Lord, Lord, open to us. But he answered and said, Verily I say unto you, I know you not. Watch therefore, for ye know neither the day nor the hour wherein the Son of man cometh. (Matthew 25:11–13)

Scripture establishes the fact that we cannot neglect so great a salvation and still think we can get in if we miss the Rapture. I want us to look at the last few verses in

Matthew 24. After giving all these signs that would occur before His return, He drove the point home with these last few verses.

> **Therefore be ye also ready: for in such an hour as ye think not the Son of man cometh. Who then is a faithful and wise servant, whom his lord hath made ruler over his household, to give them meat in due season? Blessed [is] that servant, whom his lord when he cometh shall find so doing. Verily I say unto you, That he shall make him ruler over all his goods. But and if that evil servant shall say in his heart, My lord delayeth his coming; And shall begin to smite [his] fellowservants, and to eat and drink with the drunken;**

> **The lord of that servant shall come in a day when he looketh not for [him], and in an hour that he is not aware of, And shall cut him asunder, and appoint [him] his portion with the hypocrites: there shall be weeping and gnashing of teeth. (Matthew 24:44–51)**

Matthew 24 winds up with a parable of a servant. The Lord made clear that if that servant is found to be wise and faithful when Jesus returns, he will be richly blessed and rewarded. However, if he is found to be unfaithful, he will be put in the same place as the hypocrites: there shall be weeping and gnashing of teeth.

If people are not ready when the Rapture takes place, they will wind up in hell with the hypocrites. Very highly educated people have debated Matthew 24 for years. I have listened to what some have said and even studied some of their charts. I claim to know only what the Spirit of God has shown me. The main thing I get is that we don't know the day or the hour, so we must be ready; if we are not, we will wind up with the hypocrites in hell. If we miss the Rapture, the door will be shut just as the door of the ark was shut by the Lord Himself. Get ready.

The main prerequisite for the return of Christ and the end of the church age—this generation—is when the gospel has been preached to all nations.

And this gospel of the kingdom shall be preached in all the world for a witness unto all nations; and then shall the end come. (Matthew 24:14)

Jesus's main focus throughout this chapter is for us to be ready for His return because we do not know when it will be. We need to be found as faithful and wise servants. After Jesus gave all these signs that are coming on earth, he began verse 33 with parables to help all His points sink in.

> **So likewise ye, when ye shall see all these things, know that it** [the rapture] **is near, [even] at the doors. Verily I say unto you, This generation** [the Church age] **shall not pass, till all these things be fulfilled. Heaven and earth shall pass away, but my words shall not pass away. But of that day and hour** [of the Rapture] **knoweth no [man], no, not the angels of heaven, but my Father only. (Matthew 24:33–36)**

The last verse in this chapter leaves us with the conclusion that the unfaithful servants will wind up with the hypocrites. Jesus never gave us any hope that the disobedient would have a second chance to get into heaven after the Rapture; that is humanity's theology, and it doesn't agree with scripture. So why do so many books and movies give people the false hope that it is okay to disobey God? Some of these books and movies leave people with the false idea that God mockers, adulterers, and even false prophets can still get into heaven even after they miss the Rapture.

I know how many times God has corrected me through His grace and mercy; I do not want His wrath and judgment to fall on anyone. I do, however, want people to take a close look at what they have been taught and compare it to the scriptures.

No matter what Bible prophecy teacher you follow, the only one who knows everything is Jesus; He is the only one who can never be wrong. But even Jesus himself doesn't know when He is coming back; only the Father knows that. So be ready; don't play games with God.

The idea that people who reject the great salvation provided by the cross of Christ can still get into heaven after the Rapture goes back to the devil's first lie—that it is okay to disobey God. This false theology rests on a misinterpretation of where the Rapture is recorded in Revelation. Do you know where the teacher you follow says the Rapture is recorded in the Bible?

In the next chapter, we will take a close look at where the Rapture is recorded in the scripture. Please base what you believe on the Bible, not on my opinion or anybody else's. We will all be judged according to our works and by the Word of God.

Please understand that the Bible teaches us to be ready for the Rapture. Jesus gave no hope for a second chance. The door will be shut after that (Matthew 25:10).

Chapter 4

Saved from God's Wrath

M ost theologians say that there are three views on the
Rapture—pre-tribulation, mid-tribulation, or post-
tribulation. I do not use any of these terms; I believe in
what I call the pre-wrath of God Rapture. God will never
pour His wrath out on His children! I believe that if we
start categorizing times and seasons too much, we will be
hung up in trying to figure out too many things that Jesus
specifically said weren't any of our business. We can get
hung up on things that God has put in His own power.
These things are not for us to know. We are to be more
concerned with fulfilling the Great Commission than
trying to figure what nation this or that symbol represents.
I am not saying that God would have us ignorant; anyone
who reads the Bible and looks at the news has to know the
end is nearer now than ever. Our focus must be winning
the lost, not trying to figure out times and seasons.

When they therefore were come together, they asked of him, saying, Lord, wilt thou at this time restore again the kingdom to Israel? And he said unto them, It is not for you to know the times or the seasons, which the Father hath put in his own power.

But ye shall receive power, after that the Holy Ghost is come upon you: and ye shall be witnesses unto me both in Jerusalem, and in all Judaea, and in Samaria, and unto the uttermost part of the earth. And when he had spoken these things, while they beheld, he was taken up; and a cloud received him out of their sight. (Acts 1:6–9)

The last thing Jesus said to His disciples before He ascended to heaven was that it was not for us to know the times and seasons. So let's not get hung up on graphs and charts or man's theology. Let's stay filled with power that comes from the precious Holy Spirit and be effective witnesses who carry out the Great Commission in these last days.

Revelation 4:1 is the most widely held scripture for the Rapture happening found in Revelation. This is where the pre-tribulation teachers say the Rapture will take place. These teachers have published best-selling books, movies, and Bibles. These publications have left people with the idea that they can reject Christ and still get into heaven after the Rapture. Let's take a close look at the verse that they say is the Rapture.

> **After this I looked, and, behold, a door [was] opened in heaven: and the first voice which I heard [was] as it were of a trumpet talking with me; which said, Come up hither, and I will shew thee things which must be hereafter. (Revelation 4:1)**

The Bible says this is a call to John only to come up and see the things that are yet to come; it is not a call to the entire church. If you believe that this is the Rapture, you can believe people can reject Christ, live any way they want, and still make it to heaven (as some books and movies depict).

Now, we will take a look at the scripture where the Rapture does take place in Revelation.

> **And I looked, and behold a white cloud, and upon the cloud [one] sat like unto the Son of man, having on his head a golden crown, and in his hand a sharp sickle. And another angel came out of the temple, crying with a loud voice to him that sat on the cloud, Thrust in thy sickle, and reap:**

41

> **for the time is come for thee to reap;**
> **for the harvest of the earth is ripe.**
> **And he that sat on the cloud thrust in**
> **his sickle on the earth; and the earth**
> **was reaped. (Revelation 14:14–16)**

If you have certain study Bibles, you will see on the heading of the page where this previous verse is that they state this is the Battle of Armageddon. You will also find they put it in again. They will have the same heading over the page where the Battle of Armageddon actually does take place in scripture. Here is the verse in which the Battle of Armageddon is definitely recorded as happening in Revelation.

> **And I saw heaven opened, and behold**
> **a white horse; and he that sat upon**
> **him [was] called Faithful and True,**
> **and in righteousness he doth judge**
> **and make war. (Revelation 19:11)**

For Revelation 4:1 to be the Rapture, you have to put the Battle of Armageddon in Revelation twice. I don't know everything about this book, but I know Revelation 4:1 is not the Rapture. You are left with deciding which verse you believe is the Rapture—Revelation 4:1 or Revelation 14:14–16. It should be clear that Revelation 4:1 is a call to John only; it should also be clear that Revelation 14:14–16 is a call for Jesus to reap the earth.

Now, we will look again at Revelation 14:14–16; I want you to see what is meant when I use the phrase pre-wrath of God.

> **And I looked, and behold a white cloud, and upon the cloud [one] sat like unto the Son of man, having on his head a golden crown, and in his hand a sharp sickle. And another angel came out of the temple, crying with a loud voice to him that sat on the cloud, Thrust in thy sickle, and reap: for the time is come for thee to reap; for the harvest of the earth is ripe. And he that sat on the cloud thrust in his sickle on the earth; and the earth was reaped. (Revelation 14:14–16)**

John said that the one who sat on the cloud looked like the Son of Man, Jesus. John would certainly know what He looked like. We also see that an angel was coming out of the temple with direct orders from God the Father to the Son of Man to reap the earth. The reaping we see in these verses is the Rapture; there is nothing negative about it. Those who will be reaped will be saved from the wrath of God (1 Thessalonians 1:10) that is to come. The wrath of Satan doesn't compare to God's.

Now we will look at Revelation 14:17–20.

And another angel came out of the temple which is in heaven, he also having a sharp sickle. And another angel came out from the altar, which had power over fire; and cried with a loud cry to him that had the sharp sickle, saying, Thrust in thy sharp sickle, and gather the clusters of the vine of the earth; for her grapes are fully ripe. And the angel thrust in his sickle into the earth, and gathered the vine of the earth, and cast [it] into the great winepress of the wrath of God. And the winepress was trodden without the city, and blood came out of the winepress, even unto the horse bridles, by the space of a thousand [and] six hundred furlongs. (Revelation 14:17–20)

It should be very clear by reading these verses that these are two different occurrences. One is reaped to be saved from the wrath to come (Revelation 14:14–16). The latter is cast into the great wine press of the wrath of God (Revelation 14:17–20).

The wrath of God begins in Revelation 15:1.

And I saw another sign in heaven, great and marvelous, seven angels

having the seven last plagues; for in them is filled up the wrath of God. (Revelation 15:1)

God will never pour His wrath out on His children. I pray that you will be ready when the Son of Man reaps the earth. If you don't go up in the Rapture, sudden destruction will come upon you and you will not escape.

But of the times and the seasons, brethren, ye have no need that I write unto you. 2 For yourselves know perfectly that the day of the Lord so cometh as a thief in the night. 3 For when they shall say, Peace and safety; then sudden destruction cometh upon them, as travail upon a woman with child; and they shall not escape. (1 Thessalonians 5:1–3)

I hope by reading this chapter that you see God will get His children out before He pours His wrath out on the earth. God will not allow us to be tempted without making a way for us to escape it (1 Corinthians 10:13). We must always base our belief on the Bible. We cannot give more credence to books or movies than we do to the Word of God.

The devil is constantly seeking whom he may devour. His mission is to steal, kill, and destroy; he is always looking to deceive. The core of all of the devil's lies will in some form or another be, "You can disobey God and get by with it." This is the idea that the most popular Rapture movies and books leave you with. I personally know people who will give these books and movies to friends, even children and grandchildren. They are trying to show them how to get to heaven after they have missed the Rapture. This is a false hope and contradicts scripture. The Bible plainly says that day shall come on them as a thief and that they shall not escape it (1 Thessalonians 5:1–3). After Jesus gets His bride, the door will be shut (Matthew 25:10).

I hope and pray all people will ask God's forgiveness and teach others to remain faithful to Christ. If they do not understand what the Bible speaks on these things and have misled others, I pray God will grant them repentance through acknowledging the truth.

> **In meekness instructing those that oppose themselves; if God peradventure will give them repentance to the acknowledging of the truth; 26 And [that] they may recover themselves out of the snare of the devil, who are taken captive by him at his will. (2 Timothy 2:25–26)**

Now, we need to look at other verses in Matthew 24 that will take place before the Rapture. As we look at what Jesus said in Matthew 24:1–32, we see all these signs coming to pass and will know the Rapture is close—even at the door.

> **So likewise ye, when ye shall see all these things, know that it** [the Rapture] **[is near, [even] at the doors. Verily I say unto you, This generation** [the church age] **shall not pass, till all these things be fulfilled. (Matthew 24:33–34)**

It is very clear that when we see all these things, we will know the Rapture is near. We should be found faithful to God at all times and thus be ready for the Rapture. Let us not get hung up on trying to figure out the times and seasons.

> **When ye therefore shall see the abomination of desolation, spoken of by Daniel the prophet, stand in the holy place, (whoso readeth, let him understand.) (Matthew 24:15)**

The third temple must be rebuilt in Jerusalem before this can take place. I pray you will not think you can wait until you see the construction begin on the temple to surrender your life to Christ. This would be just as much a game as thinking you could get into heaven after rejecting the gospel and missing the Rapture. Let us all be found faithfully serving God when Jesus returns for His bride.

There is coming a time when a false sense of peace will be seen in the world. It will be a time when people will say that Jesus is not the only way to the Father. It will be a time when even leaders of the so-called Christian Church will want to support the Jews who rebuild the third temple and even reinstate blood sacrifice. This will be an abomination to God. This will be seen by the world as freedom of religion. True Christians will be hated above all nations for not giving them their blessing.

Too many times, so-called Christians compromise their faith in the name of peace. We should be peacemakers but never at the expense of truth.

> **Think not that I am come to send peace on earth: I came not to send peace, but a sword. (Matthew 10:34)**

Too many times, people hold the U.S. Constitution above the Word of God. They are willing to fight you over the right for Muslims to build mosques or Jews to reinstate blood sacrifice. We must never give them our blessing in doing such things. If we do, we are partaking of their evil deeds.

> **Whosoever transgresseth, and abideth not in the doctrine of Christ, hath not God. He that abideth in the doctrine of Christ, he hath both the Father and the Son. If there come any unto you, and bring not this doctrine,**

receive him not into [your] house, neither bid him God speed: For he that biddeth him God speed [blesses his efforts] **is partaker of his evil deeds. (2 John 1:9–11)**

There has been a very strong push as long as I can remember for blessing the Jewish people. We need to understand that without the Jews, our Christian faith would not even be here. Thank God for the Jews; we should bless them for being the people God used to reveal Himself to the world. They are the physical linage that our soon returning King, Jesus, came through. We should use this historical fact to try to save them. They need to understand, however, that they must be born again; their linage alone will not get them into heaven.

Jesus told Nicodemus in John 3 that he had to be born again of the Spirit of God. To be a Pharisee, you had to have the right physical linage. Nicodemus qualified for this position, but his linage did not qualify him for heaven.

There was a man of the Pharisees, named Nicodemus, a ruler of the Jews: The same came to Jesus by night, and said unto him, Rabbi, we know that thou art a teacher come from God: for no man can do these miracles that thou doest, except God be with him. Jesus answered and said

unto him, Verily, verily, I say unto thee, Except a man be born again, he cannot see the kingdom of God. (John 3:1–3)

It is very clear that the Jews' linage does not qualify them for heaven. If they reject Jesus Christ, they will not go to heaven. If they are trusting in being born of the flesh, they have no chance.

He came unto his own, and his own received him not. But as many as received him, to them gave he power to become the sons of God, [even] to them that believe on his name: Which were born, not of blood, nor of the will of the flesh, nor of the will of man, but of God. (John 1:11–13)

I am emphasizing this because there will soon be a push to help the Jews rebuild the third temple in Jerusalem. I believe this push will come from the government of the United States and other countries; it will even receive support from many prominent Christian leaders. In doing this, they will be supporting a reinstating of blood sacrifice, a tremendous offense to God. The first animal they will sacrifice will be a perfect red heifer. According to Jewish tradition, they must do this for purification before construction can begin. But we must be cautious not to fall into this push for supporting the Jews in reinstating blood sacrifice. If we do, we will be just as guilty as they are in saying that the blood of Jesus was not enough.

> **Whosoever transgresseth, and abideth not in the doctrine of Christ, hath not God. He that abideth in the doctrine of Christ, he hath both the Father and the Son. If there come any unto you, and bring not this doctrine, receive him not into [your] house, neither bid him God speed: For he that biddeth him God speed is partaker of his evil deeds. (2 John 1:9–11)**

We must be cautious not to fall into this abomination. We must have a biblical view of the Jews who reject this great salvation provided by the cross of Christ. We will look at some verses of Jesus dealing with Jews who rejected Him.

> **I know that ye are Abraham's seed;** [physical seed] **but ye seek to kill me, because my word hath no place in you. I speak that which I have seen with my Father: and ye do that which ye have seen with your father. They answered and said unto him, Abraham is our father. Jesus saith unto them, If ye were Abraham's**

children, ye would do the works of Abraham. ... Jesus said unto them, If God were your Father, ye would love me: for I proceeded forth and came from God; neither came I of myself, but he sent me. Why do ye not understand my speech? [even] because ye cannot hear my word. Ye are of [your] father the devil, and the lusts of your father ye will do. He was a murderer from the beginning, and abode not in the truth, because there is no truth in him. When he speaketh a lie, he speaketh of his own: for he is a liar, and the father of it. (John 8:37–39, 42–44)

These verses make clear what Jesus knew about the Jews who rejected Him. Jesus was sent only to the Jews. Of all nations, the Jews had the opportunity to receive the gospel first.

But he answered and said, I am not sent but unto the lost sheep of the house of Israel. (Matthew 15:24)

However, His own people did not receive Him.

He came unto his own, and his own received him not. (John 1:11)

Though they did not receive Him, they are not cast off forever. God is able to graft them in again if they accept Christ.

> **And they also, if they abide not still in unbelief, shall be grafted in: for God is able to graft them in again. (Romans 11:23)**

God wills for the Jews to be saved along with everybody else. We hear the heart of God toward the Jewish nation through the apostle Paul.

> **Brethren, my heart's desire and prayer to God for Israel is, that they might be saved. For I bear them record that they have a zeal of God, but not according to knowledge. For they being ignorant of God's righteousness, and going about to establish their own righteousness, have not submitted themselves unto the righteousness of God. (Romans 10:1–3)**

Jesus told us how to respond to people, including Jews, who reject the gospel.

> **And whosoever will not receive you, when ye go out of that city, shake off**

> **the very dust from your feet for a testimony against them. (Luke 9:5)**

Shaking the dust off your feet is saying, "I wash my hands of you. I have done what God requires of me concerning you. I cannot waste any more of my time with you." A big part of our testimony to them is letting them know how serious it is to reject Jesus. The apostle Paul understood this principle established by Jesus.

> **But when the Jews saw the multitudes, they were filled with envy, and spake against those things which were spoken by Paul, contradicting and blaspheming. Then Paul and Barnabas waxed bold, and said, It was necessary that the word of God should first have been spoken to you: but seeing ye put it from you, and judge yourselves unworthy of everlasting life, lo, we turn to the Gentiles. ... But the Jews stirred up the devout and honourable women, and the chief men of the city, and raised persecution against Paul and Barnabas, and expelled them out of their coasts. But they shook off the dust of their feet against them, and came unto Iconium. And the disciples**

were filled with joy, and with the Holy Ghost. (Acts 13:45–46, 50–52)

It is imperative that we understand God's view of people who reject the gospel, including Jews. There is today an extreme hard push for a one-world religion; it is reflected in how even prominent Christian leaders push the physical linage and faith of the Jews. I agree that Israel should have all the land God gave the Jews in the Bible, but the Jews who do not accept Jesus as Messiah do not have God the Father. If they reject Christ, we are not to even bid them God's speed much less help them build the third temple and reinstate the blood sacrifice.

The spiritual Jews are those who accept Jesus Christ by faith.

For he is not a Jew, which is one outwardly; neither[is that] circumcision, which is outward in the flesh: But he [is] a Jew, which is one inwardly; and circumcision [is that] of the heart, in the spirit, [and] not in the letter; whose praise [is] not of men, but of God. (Romans 2:28–29)

Not as though the word of God hath taken none effect. For they [are] not all Israel, which are of Israel: Neither, because they are the seed of Abraham, [are they] all children:

but, In Isaac shall thy seed be called. (Romans 9:6–7)

Anyone can become a true spiritual child of Abraham by faith in Christ.

Know ye therefore that they which are of faith, the same are the children of Abraham. ... So then they which be of faith are blessed with faithful Abraham. ... For ye are all the children of God by faith in Christ Jesus. ... And if ye [be] Christ's, then are ye Abraham's seed, and heirs according to the promise. (Galatians 3:7, 9, 26, 29)

We have established based on scripture that we cannot put our stamp of approval on any religion other than Christianity. The spiritual Jews are those who have faith in Christ.

I believe by studying the Bible that construction on the third temple in Jerusalem will begin very soon; it will be built near the dome of the rock, the Muslim holy place. Most people around the globe will be glad to see that happen. It will even be strongly pushed by so-called Christian leaders. They will say, "Finally, there is peace in the Holy City." They will say, "Finally, different faiths are no longer divided." One man will be a key player in this effort; he will keep peace among the different faiths that have been divided against each other for so long. Most of the people on earth will be worshiping him as their god and not even realize it.

Christians will be expected to say that Jesus is a way to the Father but not the only way. Christians will be expected to worship alongside faiths that reject Jesus as the Messiah. True Christians will be hated above all nations for keeping the testimony of Jesus. The persecution of Christians will be the worst the world has ever known. One of the men who will be helping this effort will be the Antichrist. At some point, he will sit in the third temple, put an end to the sacrifice, and claim to be god (Daniel 9:27, 12:11; Matthew 24:15). We are about to look at 2 Thessalonians 2: 1-12. These verses give us a clear understanding of what must happen before the coming of our Lord Jesus Christ.

Now we beseech you, brethren, by the coming of our Lord Jesus Christ, and [by] our gathering together unto him, That ye be not soon shaken in mind, or be troubled, neither by spirit, nor by word, nor by letter as from us, as that the day of Christ is at hand. Let no man deceive you by any means: for [that day shall not come], except there come a falling away first, and that man of sin be revealed, the son of perdition; Who opposeth and exalteth himself above

all that is called God, or that is worshipped; so that he as God itteth in the temple of God, shewing himself that he is God. Remember ye not, that, when I was yet with you, I told you these things? And now ye know what withholdeth that he might be revealed in his time. For the mystery of iniquity doth already work: only he who now letteth [will let], until he be taken out of the way. And then shall that Wicked be revealed, whom the Lord shall consume With the spirit of his mouth, and shall destroy with the brightness of his coming: [Even him], whose coming is after the working of Satan with all power and signs and lying wonders, And with all deceivableness of unrighteousness in them that perish; because they received not the love of the truth, that they might be saved. And for this cause God shall send them strong delusion, that they should believe a lie: That they all might be damned who believed not the truth, but had pleasure in unrighteousness. (2Th 2:1-12 KJV)

We see here in these first verses that the Apostle Paul is concerned about his church's state of mind. Evidently there had been at least one forged letter circulating that had supposedly been written by the Apostle Paul. This forged letter left the church in Thessalonica with the idea that the Rapture had already occurred. Paul told them that the rapture would not come until there was a great falling away and the Antichrist was revealed. These Christians could have easily been led away in thinking that Jesus was already setting up his kingdom in another place, possibly Jerusalem. Jesus warned of this in Mathew 24.

> **Then if any man shall say unto you, Lo, here [is] Christ, or there; believe [it] not. ...Wherefore if they shall say unto you, Behold, he is in the desert; go not forth: behold, [he is] in the secret chambers; believe [it] not. For as the lightning cometh out of the east, and shineth even unto the west; so shall also the coming of the Son of man be. (Mat 24:23, 26-27 KJV)**

When Jesus comes back on the clouds there will be no mistake about it, [Rev.1:7] every eye will see him. I am looking forward to that day with great anticipation.

Now to the mater of what is holding back the Antichrist from coming into power. Most pre-tribulation teachers say it is the Church. Thank God that the Church is making a difference. Thank God the gates of hell will not prevail against the true Church of Jesus Christ. Thank God that he always causes us to triumph. But is the Church what is holding back the Antichrist? If the Church is holding back the Antichrist and his agenda, why are abortion clinics still operating in America? Why has prayer been taken out of schools? Why has the definition of marriage been changed? Why has the Ten Commandments been removed from the court house wall? Why have we changed the sign over the bathroom door? Why are main line denominations performing same sex marriages and even ordaining openly homosexual ministers? It is because in a democratically run society the majority makes the rules they want to follow. When that majority refuses to obey the Word of God sin runs rampant. One day God will make them pay for their rebellion against Him if they do not repent. My hope and prayer is for preachers to stand up in the pulpit and take a stand against sin, not give their congregation an excuse to stay in it.

It is Michael and His angels that is keeping the Spirit of Antichrist from possessing the man that will fulfill that role. The Antichrist will not come into power until God gives the order for Michael to be taken out of the way (2nd Th. 2:7). We see a picture of this battle in the heavens in the book of Revelation.

And there was war in heaven: Michael and his angels fought against the dragon; and the dragon fought and

his angels, And prevailed not; neither was their place found any more in heaven. And the great dragon was cast out, that old serpent, called the Devil, and Satan, which deceiveth the whole world: he was cast out into the earth, and his angels were cast out with him. And I heard a loud voice saying in heaven, Now is come salvation, and strength, and the kingdom of our God, and the power of his Christ: for the accuser of our brethren is cast down, which accused them before our God day and night. And they overcame him by the blood of the Lamb, and by the word of their testimony; and they loved not their lives unto the death. Therefore rejoice, [ye] heavens, and ye that dwell in them. Woe to the inhabiters of the earth and of the sea! for the devil is come down unto you, having great wrath, because he knoweth that he hath but a short time. (Rev 12:7-12 KJV)

I have heard people that I love and respect say that any Christian worth his salt could cast the devil out of the Antichrist. It is true that there is deliverance in the name of Jesus. We do have power over the enemy in Jesus name. However we cannot be duped into thinking we can super imposed our will over someone else`s. We will never be able to cast a demon out of a willing vessel. The person must desire to be free of the demon.

I want to reemphasize that it is not for us to know the times and seasons that God has put in His own power. Our part is to be led by the Spirit of God and not be led astray with every wind of doctrine by the sleight of others. Our focus should be on being filled with the power of the Holy Ghost and being effective witnesses in these last days.

We need to recognize that the devil in some form will try to get us to compromise the Word of God. The only way we will be able to discern the truth from lies is by being filled with the Holy Spirit and by reading, studying, knowing, and doing what the Bible says. We must live by every Word that proceeds out of the mouth of God, not by every word of our favorite preachers.

We must recognize that the core of all the devil's lies is this: "It's okay if I disobey God." The devil would have you believe you can reject the gospel, miss the Rapture, and still get into heaven. Scripture plainly states that after Jesus gets His bride, the door will be shut just as was the door on Noah's ark.

And while they went to buy, the bridegroom came; and they that were ready went in with him to the

marriage: and the door was shut. (Matthew 25:10)

The Rapture will come as a thief in the night, and the rejecters of the gospel will not escape.

For yourselves know perfectly that the day of the Lord so cometh as a thief in the night. For when they shall say, Peace and safety; then sudden destruction cometh upon them, as travail upon a woman with child; and they shall not escape. (1 Thessalonians 5:2–3)

The unfaithful servants will have their place with the hypocrites.

The lord of that servant shall come in a day when he looketh not for [him], and in an hour that he is not aware of, And shall cut him asunder, and appoint [him] his portion with the hypocrites: there shall be weeping and gnashing of teeth. (Matthew 24:50–51)

Chapter 5

Every Eye Shall See Him

Even if after reading this book, you do not agree with everything that has been said, I urge you to agree with this: We need to be ready when Jesus returns to get His bride. We must not play games with God. We must base our belief solely upon the Bible.

> **Be ye therefore ready also: for the Son of man cometh at an hour when ye think not. (Luke 12:40)**

He is coming back just as He left, on the clouds.

> **And when he had spoken these things, while they beheld, he was taken up; and a cloud received him out of their sight. And while they**

looked stedfastly toward heaven as he went up, behold, two men stood by them in white apparel; Which also said, Ye men of Galilee, why stand ye gazing up into heaven? this same Jesus, which is taken up from you into heaven, shall so come in like manner as ye have seen him go into heaven. (Acts 1:9–11)

They saw Him going with the clouds, and every eye will see Him coming with the clouds.

Behold, he cometh with clouds; and every eye shall see him, and they [also] which pierced him: and all kindreds of the earth shall wail because of him. Even so, Amen. (Revelation 1:7)

It is essential that we understand that the Rapture will not be a secret happening. The dead in Christ will rise first, and then, we will be changed to meet the Lord in the air, where every eye will see Him. There will likely be all types of false theories about what has taken place. Some will likely say that extraterrestrials have studied our religion and imitated what they found. They would likely say these aliens will come back later and take over the planet. But it will be Jesus Himself.

In a moment, in the twinkling of an eye, at the last trump: for the trumpet shall sound, and the dead shall be raised incorruptible, and we shall be changed. (1 Corinthians 15:52)

For the Lord himself shall descend from heaven with a shout, with the voice of the archangel, and with the trump of God: and the dead in Christ shall rise first. Then we which are alive [and] remain shall be caught up together with them in the clouds, to meet the Lord in the air: and so shall we ever be with the Lord. (1 Thessalonians 4:16–17)

Every eye will see Him at this point, even those that pierced Him thousands of years before. The Bible refers to the dead in hell being able to see and understand what is going on in heaven and on earth. We find the perfect example of this in the story of the rich man and Lazarus in Luke 16:19–31. We also find in Revelation that the martyrs in heaven are aware of what is going on in the earth.

And when he had opened the fifth seal, I saw under the altar the souls of them that were slain for the word of God, and for the testimony which they held: And they cried with a loud

> **voice, saying, How long, O Lord,
> holy and true, dost thou not judge
> and avenge our blood on them that
> dwell on the earth? And white robes
> were given unto every one of them;
> and it was said unto them, that they
> should rest yet for a little season,
> until their fellowservants also and
> their brethren, that should be killed
> as they [were], should be fulfilled.
> (Revelation 6:9–11)**

So why is it important to understand the Rapture
will be visible to everyone? It is because if you believe it
is secret or invisible, you could be easily led astray. You
could be led into thinking that the Rapture had already
occurred and then be deceived into going after a false
Christ.

> **Then if any man shall say unto you, Lo,
> here [is] Christ, or there; believe [it]
> not. For there shall arise false Christs,
> and false prophets, and shall shew
> great signs and wonders; insomuch
> that, if [it were] possible, they shall
> deceive the very elect. Behold, I have
> told you before. Wherefore if they
> shall say unto you, Behold, he is in
> the desert; go not forth: behold, [he**

**is] in the secret chambers; believe [it]
not. For as the lightning cometh out
of the east, and shineth even unto the
west; so shall also the coming of the
Son of man be. (Matthew 24:23–27)**

When Jesus comes back to get His bride, every eye
will see Him. His returning will light up the earth. When
Jesus comes to get us, He will be as visible as the sun and
much more powerful. His coming will be with great glory.

**And then shall appear the sign of the
Son of man in heaven: and then shall
all the tribes of the earth mourn, and
they shall see the Son of man coming
in the clouds of heaven with power
and great glory. (Matthew 24:30)**

We must believe that His coming will be with power
and great glory and that everyone will see Him. If we
don't, we might believe He is here or in the desert or in
the secret chambers and try to find Him. He's coming to
reap the earth on a cloud, the same way He left. Everyone
will see Him.

**Behold, he cometh with clouds; and
every eye shall see him, and they [also]
which pierced him: and all kindreds
of the earth shall wail because of
him. Even so, Amen. (Revelation 1:7)**

> **And I looked, and behold a white cloud, and upon the cloud [one] sat like unto the Son of man, having on his head a golden crown, and in his hand a sharp sickle. And another angel came out of the temple, crying with a loud voice to him that sat on the cloud, Thrust in thy sickle, and reap: for the time is come for thee to reap; for the harvest of the earth is ripe. And he that sat on the cloud thrust in his sickle on the earth; and the earth was reaped. (Revelation 14:14–16)**

When Jesus comes back to smite the nations, He will be on a white horse, not a cloud.

> **And I saw heaven opened, and behold a white horse; and he that sat upon him [was] called Faithful and True, and in righteousness he doth judge and make war. His eyes [were] as a flame of fire, and on his head [were] many crowns; and he had a name written, that no man knew, but he himself. And he [was] clothed with a vesture dipped in blood: and his name is called The Word of God. And**

the armies [which were] in heaven followed him upon white horses, clothed in fine linen, white and clean. (Revelation 19:11–14)

It is my hope and prayer that after reading this book and studying the scriptures, you will be encouraged to remain faithful to Christ and will encourage others to do the same. I am confident as you are finishing up, you will be determined to find God's will and purpose for your life and fulfill it.

Jesus is coming back in a little while. May we be found faithfully fulfilling His purpose in our lives.

For yet a little while, and he that shall come will come, and will not tarry. Now the just shall live by faith: but if [any man] draw back, my soul shall have no pleasure in him. But we are not of them who draw back unto perdition; but of them that believe to the saving of the soul. (Hebrews 10:37–39)

No person—no matter who they are, no matter how educated they are—can know everything about Revelation; it can be understood only as the Spirit of God reveals it. I certainly do not claim to know everything about Bible prophecy or any other subject in the Bible for that matter.

**For we know in part, and we prophesy
in part. (1 Corinthians 13:9)**

There are however some major points that should
be plainly and simply understood by reading this book
and studying scriptures given in it. I offer these in the
following conclusion.

Conclusion

First, we must base our belief on scripture. We cannot put anyone's doctrine above the Word of God. We need people anointed of God to help teach us and lead us to truth. They are, however, never the final authority. No matter who they are, people can be wrong. We should always be willing to give others grace. If, however, they are changing the fundamentals of the gospel, we need to refuse them and their teaching. No matter how charismatic they are and how much we enjoy their style of teaching, we must know what the Word of God says and live by that.

> These [things] have I written unto you concerning them that seduce you. But the anointing which ye have received of him abideth in you, and ye need not that any man teach you: but as the same anointing teacheth you of all things, and is truth, and is no

> **lie, and even as it hath taught you, ye
> shall abide in him. (1 John 2:26–27)**

A large following doesn't always mean a preacher is biblically sound.

> **Because strait [is] the gate, and
> narrow [is] the way, which leadeth
> unto life, and few there be that find
> it. (Matthew 7:14)**

Second, we need to be able to recognize the deception of the Antichrist. No matter how cleverly and subtly the devil's lies start, they will lead to this ending: you can reject the gospel, live disobediently toward God, and still get into heaven even after missing the Rapture.

Third, no one knows the day or the hour of the Rapture, not even Jesus.

> **But of that day and hour knoweth no
> [man], no, not the angels of heaven,
> but my Father only. (Matthew 24:36)**

I would never listen to anyone who starts setting a date for the Rapture; this includes any date even after the third temple is built in Jerusalem. Jesus said it was not for us to know the times and seasons.

> **And he said unto them, It is not for
> you to know the times or the seasons,**

which the Father hath put in his own power. (Acts 1:7)

Fourth, we must be ready when Jesus comes for His bride. We must not think we can safely put off being saved and submitting the lordship of our lives to Jesus. We cannot think that we can live in our fleshly desires and still get to heaven after missing the Rapture even if we think God will show special favor to the Jews and let the 144,000 in after the Rapture. What has that got to do with us? Let us all be ready when he returns.

And what I say unto you I say unto all, Watch. (Mark 13:37)

We cannot think we can be found unfaithful and still get into to heaven after missing the Rapture. If we are found unfaithful, we will be appointed our portion with unbelievers.

But and if that servant say in his heart, My lord delayeth his coming; and shall begin to beat the menservants and maidens, and to eat and drink, and to be drunken; The lord of that servant will come in a day when he looketh not for [him], and at an hour when he is not aware, and will cut him in sunder, and will appoint him

his portion with the unbelievers. (Luke 12:45–46)

As the bride of Christ, we must be ready with our lamps filled with oil and trimmed and burning when the Bridegroom comes for us. If we miss the Rapture, the door will be shut.

And while they went to buy, the bridegroom came; and they that were ready went in with him to the marriage: and the door was shut. (Matthew 25:10)

Even if they call Him Lord and try to get in after the Rapture, Jesus will say, "I don't know you."

Afterward came also the other virgins, saying, Lord, Lord, open to us. But he answered and said, Verily I say unto you, I know you not. Watch therefore, for ye know neither the day nor the hour wherein the Son of man cometh. (Matthew 25:11–13)

I Jesus have sent mine angel to testify unto you these things in the churches. I am the root and the offspring of David, [and] the bright and morning star. And the Spirit and

**the bride say, Come. And let him that
heareth say, Come. And let him that
is athirst come. And whosoever will,
let him take the water of life freely.
For I testify unto every man that
heareth the words of the prophecy of
this book, If any man shall add unto
these things, God shall add unto him
the plagues that are written in this
book: And if any man shall take away
from the words of the book of this
prophecy, God shall take away his
part out of the book of life, and out
of the holy city, and [from] the things
which are written in this book. He
which testifieth these things saith,
Surely I come quickly. Amen. Even
so, come, Lord Jesus. The grace of
our Lord Jesus Christ [be] with you
all. Amen. (Revelation 22:16–21)**

It is a very serious offense to God for us to add or take
away from the Holy Bible. God magnifies His Word and
above all His name.

**I will worship toward thy holy
temple, and praise thy name for thy
lovingkindness and for thy truth: for**

thou hast magnified thy word above all thy name. (Psalm 138:2)

There is reason I have put my words in regular print and the Word of God in bold for this book. I have a respect for the Word of God. I want you to have respect for the Word of God as well. We must live by every word that proceeds out of the mouth of God. We should never make more time for others' opinions than we do for reading the Bible. No matter who the authors are, including me, they could be wrong.

Fifth, deception is abounding in these last days and is increasing faster than ever. Christians are being led away in large crowds by the errors of the wicked. Some people are no longer willing to take time to pray, read the Bible, and let the Spirit lead them into all truth. They want to be entertained by teachers who tell them what they want to hear. They like hearing how great they are. These teachers and preachers focus primarily on what is wrong with others instead of correcting and reproving those who are listening to them lest their crowds get smaller.

I charge [thee] therefore before God, and the Lord Jesus Christ, who shall judge the quick and the dead at his appearing and his kingdom; Preach the word; be instant in season, out of season; reprove, rebuke, exhort with all longsuffering and doctrine.

For the time will come when they will not endure sound doctrine; but after their own lusts shall they heap to themselves teachers, having itching ears; And they shall turn away [their] ears from the truth, and shall be turned unto fables. (2 Timothy 4:1–4)

It has been said that there will be an end time revival, but is this what the Bible teaches? Popular, modern-day preachers will use a passage in Acts as proof of this.

But this is that which was spoken by the prophet Joel; And it shall come to pass in the last days, saith God, I will pour out of my Spirit upon all flesh: and your sons and your daughters shall prophesy, and your young men shall see visions, and your old men shall dream dreams: And on my servants and on my handmaidens I will pour out in those days of my Spirit; and they shall prophesy. (Acts 2:16–18)

Thank God that we have been living for over two thousand years in the fulfillment of Joel's prophecy. But the time has come when most people are not willing to endure sound biblical teaching (2 Timothy 4:3). People flock to teachers who say what they want to hear. We cannot give more credence to our favorite preachers than we do to the Word of God. Jesus must be the author and finisher of our faith.

As time goes on, deception will get worse and worse. I recently heard a preacher refer to 1 Corinthians 2:9 as being a jumping-off point to do whatever you felt like in church.

But as it is written, Eye hath not seen, nor ear heard, neither have entered into the heart of man, the things which God hath prepared for them that love him. (1 Corinthians 2:9)

He took this verse out of context and ran with it. The operation of the Holy Spirit will always confirm what is in the Bible. The Holy Spirit will never speak of Himself; He will confirm only what the Bible says. He will never answer any prayer addressed to Him. We should, however, honor His presence and make Him welcome in the name of Jesus. He will take only what belongs to Jesus and show it to us. He will never speak of Himself because He is not the only spirit who can speak. When any spirit speaks, it must fall in line with the written Word of God.

As I have already stated deception is bad now, but it will get worse.

But evil men and seducers shall wax worse and worse, deceiving, and being deceived. (2 Timothy 3:13)

And many false prophets shall rise, and shall deceive many. (Matthew 24:11)

Jesus asked if He would find faith on earth when he returned.

I tell you that he will avenge them speedily. Nevertheless when the Son of man cometh, shall he find faith on the earth? (Luke 18:8)

The way I understand this, true faith will be rare when He returns.

Let us not forget that the main prerequisite for the Rapture is the gospel being preached to all nations. If our presenting the gospel is not received by others, that will be used by God as a testimony against them (Matthew 10:18; Mark 6:11, 13:9). We must be found faithful in doing what we are called to do regardless of the response or the consequences.

There is coming a time when false religions will come together, a time when all faiths will be accepted as equal, a time when even so-called Christians will worship alongside other religions that say Jesus is not the only way to the Father. This is what is coming in the last days, not an end time revival. Thank God that He will always have a remnant, a few who have chosen and stayed on the narrow path that leads to life.

> **Because strait [is] the gate, and narrow [is] the way, which leadeth unto life, and few there be that find it. (Matthew 7:14)**

I am looking forward to the appearing of the Son of Man coming in the clouds of heaven to get us.

> **And then shall appear the sign of the Son of man in heaven: and then shall all the tribes of the earth mourn, and they shall see the Son of man coming in the clouds of heaven with power and great glory. 31 And he shall send his angels with a great sound of a trumpet, and they shall gather together his elect from the four winds, from one end of heaven to the other. (Matthew 24:30–31)**

We should be looking forward to the Rapture just as the churches in New Testament times were and perhaps even more so. As we allow the grace of God to continue teaching us to live holy lives, we can be ready for His appearing—our blessed hope.

> **For the grace of God that bringeth salvation hath appeared to all men, Teaching us that, denying ungodliness and worldly lusts, we**

should live soberly, righteously, and godly, in this present world; Looking for that blessed hope, and the glorious appearing of the great God and our Saviour Jesus Christ. (Titus 2:11–13)

As children of God, we should be more excited about the coming of Jesus Christ than a child is about the coming of Christmas. As a child, I was always excited about Christmas. It is still my favorite holiday. When Halloween came along, I was thinking that it wouldn't be long till Thanksgiving. When Thanksgiving came, I started getting excited because that meant Christmas was close. I would get so excited that I would ask my mother how many days it was until Christmas. She taught me how to mark off the days on the calendar.

We should always be excited about the Rapture of the church much more than we were about Christmas when we were children. We cannot mark the days until the Rapture, but just as Halloween and Thanksgiving come to pass before Christmas, when we see all these things, we can know it is near, even at the door.

So likewise ye, when ye shall see all these things, know that it is near, [even] at the doors. (Matthew 24:33)

We must be ready when Christ returns for His bride. May we never think we can get right after missing the

Rapture. We need to be found faithfully doing the work we have been called to when Jesus comes.

When I was growing up, my father would give me tasks to finish before he returned. When I knew I had finished the work to the best of my ability, I had no fear of his returning; I wanted him to see the work I had completed. I knew I would be rewarded for my efforts. I also knew that if I had goofed off and not done anything, punishment was coming. I was fearful and ashamed at his returning in those cases.

This illustration is reflective of how it will be at the return of Christ. Let none of us be fearful or ashamed at His returning.

> **And now, little children, abide in him; that, when he shall appear, we may have confidence, and not be ashamed before him at his coming. (1 John 2:28)**

Thank God that the gates of hell will not prevail against the church of God that lives by every word of God. Don't quit. Be ready.

> **But he that shall endure unto the end, the same shall be saved. (Matthew 24:13)**
>
> **And, behold, I come quickly; and my reward [is] with me, to give**

every man according as his work shall be. I am Alpha and Omega, the beginning and the end, the first and the last. Blessed [are] they that do his commandments, that they may have right to the tree of life, and may enter in through the gates into the city. For without [are] dogs, and sorcerers, and whoremongers, and murderers, and idolaters, and whosoever loveth and maketh a lie. I Jesus have sent mine angel to testify unto you these things in the churches. I am the root and the offspring of David, [and] the bright and morning star. And the Spirit and the bride say, Come. And let him that heareth say, Come. And let him that is athirst come. And whosoever will, let him take the water of life freely. (Revelation 22:12–17)

A Sinner's Prayer to Receive Eternal Life through Jesus

Father God, I come to you in the name of your Son, Jesus Christ. The Bible says, "Him that cometh to me I will in no wise cast out" (John 6:33), so I come to you knowing you will receive me. I repent all my sin. I thank you that the blood of Jesus cleanses me from all my sin (1 John 1:9). Father, your Word also says that

if thou shalt confess with thy mouth the Lord Jesus, and shalt believe in thine heart that God hath raised him from the dead, thou shalt be saved. (Romans 10:9)

So by faith, I believe this and am making Jesus Lord of my life.

For with the heart man believeth unto righteousness; and with the mouth

confession is made unto salvation. (Romans 10:10)

By the power of the Holy Spirit, I will tell others what you have done for me. Fill me with you Spirit.

For the scripture saith, Whosoever believeth on him shall not be ashamed. (Romans 10:11)

Thank you that I am saved.

Signed_____

A Christian's Prayer of Repentance

Father God, I come to you in the name of Jesus. I thank you that if I confess my sin, you will forgive them and will not remember them anymore.

> **If we confess our sins, he is faithful and just to forgive us [our] sins, and to cleanse us from all unrighteousness. (1 John 1:9)**

If I have ever left anyone with the idea that they can reject the gospel and still get into heaven after they have missed the Rapture, I ask your forgiveness now. Thank you for forgiving me for what I did in ignorance.

> **Who was before a blasphemer, and a persecutor, and injurious: but I obtained mercy, because I did [it] ignorantly in unbelief. (1 Timothy 1:13)**

I commit the rest of my life to you. I want to serve you faithfully and help others do the same. I thank you for drawing closer to me as I draw closer to you.

> **Draw nigh to God, and he will draw nigh to you. Cleanse [your] hands, [ye] sinners; and purify [your] hearts, [ye] double minded. (James 4:8)**

Your servant thanks you.

Signed_____

Personal Notes

_____

_____

_____

_____

_____

_____

_____

_____

_____

_____

_____

_____

_____

Personal Notes

_____

_____

_____

_____

_____

_____

_____

_____

_____

_____

_____

_____

Personal Notes

Personal Notes

_____

_____

_____

_____

_____

_____

_____

_____

_____

_____

_____

_____

_____

Personal Notes

Personal Notes

_____

_____

_____

_____

_____

_____

_____

_____

_____

_____

_____

_____

Personal Notes

Personal Notes

_____

_____

_____

_____

_____

_____

_____

_____

_____

_____

_____

Personal Notes

Printed in the United States
By Bookmasters